Family Pets (Revised Edition)

Lola M. Schaefer
AR B.L.: 0.9
Points: 0.5   LG

Pebble®

Family Pets

Revised
and
Updated

by Lola M. Schaefer

Consulting Editor: Gail Saunders-Smith, PhD

Capstone
press®
Mankato, Minnesota

Pebble Books are published by Capstone Press,
151 Good Counsel Drive, P.O. Box 669, Mankato, Minnesota 56002.
www.capstonepress.com

1 2 3 4 5 6 13 12 11 10 09 08

Library of Congress Cataloging-in-Publication Data
Schaefer, Lola M., 1950–
　Family pets/by Lola M. Schaefer. — Rev. and updated ed.
　p. cm. — (Pebble books. Families)
　Summary: "Simple text and photographs present family pets and how they interact
with their families" — Provided by publisher.
　Includes bibliographical references and index.
　ISBN-13: 978-1-4296-1223-4 (hardcover)
　ISBN-10: 1-4296-1223-1 (hardcover)
　ISBN-13: 978-1-4296-1752-9 (softcover)
　ISBN-10: 1-4296-1752-7 (softcover)
　1. Pets — Juvenile literature. I. Title. II. Series.
SF416.2.S32 2008
636.088'7 — dc22　　　　　　　　　　　　　　　　　　2007027091

Note to Parents and Teachers

The Families set supports national social studies standards related
to identifying family members and their roles in the family. This
book describes and illustrates family pets. The images support
early readers in understanding the text. The repetition of words
and phrases helps early readers learn new words. This book also
introduces early readers to subject-specific vocabulary words, which
are defined in the glossary section. Early readers may need some
assistance to read some words and to use the Table of Contents,
Glossary, Read More, Internet Sites, and Index sections of the book.

Table of Contents

All Kinds of Pets

Families have pets.

Some family pets live inside.

Other family pets live outside.

Betty's rabbit is a fluffy pet.

Jim's cat is a smooth pet.

Ed's ferret is a thin pet.

Terry's fish is a wet pet.

Sarah's bird is
a feathery pet.

Big and Small Pets

Steve's horse is a tall pet.

Kara's hermit crab
is a small pet.

Good Friends

Pets are good family friends.

Glossary

family — a group of people related to one another; families include parents, children, grandparents, aunts, uncles, and cousins.

ferret — a long, thin animal related to the weasel; ferrets have short legs and long tails.

fluffy — covered with soft, fine hair or feathers

hermit crab — a small animal with a hard shell, eight legs, and two claws or pincers

Read More

Keenan, Sheila. *Animals in the House: A History of Pets and People.* New York: Scholastic Nonfiction, 2007.

Schaefer, Lola. *What Does Your Pet Do?* Science about Me. Vero Beach, Fla.: Rourke, 2007.

Internet Sites

FactHound offers a safe, fun way to find Internet sites related to this book. All of the sites on FactHound have been researched by our staff.

Here's how:
1. Visit *www.facthound.com*
2. Choose your grade level.
3. Type in this book ID **1429612231** for age-appropriate sites. You may also browse subjects by clicking on letters, or by clicking on pictures and words.
4. Click on the **Fetch It** button.

FactHound will fetch the best sites for you!

Index

Betty, 7
birds, 15
cats, 9
Ed, 11
ferrets, 11
fish, 13
hermit crabs, 19

horses, 17
Jim, 9
Kara, 19
rabbit, 7
Sarah, 15
Steve, 17
Terry, 13

Word Count: 61
Grade 1
Early-Intervention Level: 10

Editorial Credits

Sarah L. Schuette, revised edition editor; Kim Brown, revised edition designer

Photo Credits

Capstone Press/Karon Dubke, all